To

From

Text by Mary Joslin
Illustrations copyright © 2002 Gail Newey
This edition copyright © 2002 Lion Publishing

The moral rights of the author and illustrator
have been asserted

Published by
Lion Publishing plc
Sandy Lane West, Oxford, England
www.lion-publishing.co.uk
ISBN 0 7459 4599 6

First edition 2002
1 3 5 7 9 10 8 6 4 2 0

Acknowledgments
Scriptures quoted from the Good News Bible
published by The Bible Societies/HarperCollins Publishers Ltd, UK
© American Bible Society 1966, 1971, 1976, 1992, used with permission.

A catalogue record for this book is available
from the British Library

Typeset in 19/26 Berkeley Oldstyle BT
Printed and bound in China

The Story of the Cross

The Stations of the Cross for Children

Mary Joslin
Illustrated by Gail Newey

LION
Children's Books

The beginnings of the story

The story of the cross is the story of a man called Jesus. It begins with a visit from an angel.

Long ago, in the little town of Nazareth, lived a girl called Mary. She was soon to be married.

Then, one day, an angel appeared to her and said, 'Peace be with you! The Lord is with you and has greatly blessed you.'

Mary was alarmed. Who was this visitor? What did the words mean?

The angel said to her, 'Don't be afraid, Mary; God has been gracious to you. You will become pregnant and give birth to a son, and you will name him Jesus. He will be great and will be called the Son of the Most High God.'

Mary was puzzled, but she agreed to do as God wanted.

An angel also spoke to Joseph, the man she was to marry, and he agreed to look after Mary and her special baby.

Months later, Mary and Joseph had to make a journey to Joseph's home town of Bethlehem. The place was crowded, and they had to shelter in a stable. There, Jesus was born. Mary used a manger as his first cradle.

Out on the hills, angels danced in the midnight sky. They sang the news to shepherds who were out watching over their sheep. They told the men that a baby had been born – the One chosen by God to bring people justice and peace.

The shepherds came and found the baby. The place where he lay was dark and bare, but everything was just as the angels had said. Surely a little part of heaven had come to earth.

The years passed, and Jesus grew up to know and love God as a child loves a good father. He learned the laws that God had given his people long ago.

'"Love the Lord your God with all your heart, with all your soul, and with all your mind." This is the greatest and the most important commandment. The second most important commandment is like it: "Love your neighbour as you love yourself."'

He understood, too, how deep was God's love. He became a preacher and teacher, travelling from one place to another to speak about God to anyone who would listen.

'Love your enemies and pray for those who persecute you, so that you may become the children of your Father in heaven. For he makes his sun to shine on bad and good people alike, and gives rain to those who do good and to those who do evil.'

People flocked to listen to Jesus. The things he said seemed good and right, and were often wrapped up in stories that were clever and funny.

He was also able to heal people with just a touch, and many were eager to see his miracles.

The religious teachers were suspicious.

'He claims to teach the laws of our people,' they muttered, 'but he and many of his followers do not seem to be keeping to our rituals and traditions.'

'Indeed he does not,' replied others. 'We have seen him heal people on the Sabbath – the day when our people are commanded to do no work.'

'So his healings cannot be miracles from God,' some argued.

Others were less sure. 'How can he work miracles of such love and goodness if he is a wrongdoer?' they puzzled.

In spite of all the good they had seen Jesus do, some people began to plot to have him put to death.

It was no easy task. Jesus had a faithful band of close disciples who were always with him. The crowds treated him as a hero.

Then one of the
disciples grew disloyal.
For a handful of silver,
the one named Judas Iscariot
told Jesus' enemies where they could
find him away from the crowds.

One night, while the disciples lay
sleeping in the shady olive grove called
Gethsemane and Jesus spent the hours
praying to God, armed men were sent
to arrest him.

Jesus was dragged before the
leaders of his people and accused of
wrongdoing. People came and told
lies. All that remained was for Jesus'
own people to persuade the Romans
who ruled their land to authorize the
death sentence: they took him to the
governor, Pontius Pilate.

One: Jesus is condemned to death

What had Jesus done?

He had come with stories and wisdom.

He had come with healing and forgiveness.

He had come to make people friends with God.

But not everyone welcomed the things he said and the things he did.

There were whispers and lies.

There was anger and spite.

Jesus was condemned to death.

Dear God,
Keep me from anger and spite.
Help me to love and forgive.
Help me to follow Jesus.

Two: Jesus is made to carry the cross

Jesus was condemned to a cruel death: nailed to a cross of wood.

Soldiers loaded the cross onto his shoulders. Although he had done no wrong he was ordered to carry his heavy load through the jeering crowd.

Dear God,
When I feel alone
and troubles weigh me down
like a heavy load,
help me to know
that I am walking with Jesus.

Three: Jesus falls the first time under the cross

Jesus walked along the narrow streets of Jerusalem,
struggling with the heavy cross.

    The pavement was rough beneath his feet.

    The guard hurried him without pity.

    He lost his footing and fell.

Dear God,
I try to follow Jesus
but sometimes I fail and fall.
May I know in my heart
that Jesus is always with me.

Four: Jesus is met by his mother

Jesus' mother Mary was in Jerusalem, following her dear son as he walked to a death he did not deserve.

The love of a mother such as Mary is for ever.

Dear God,
Thank you for the great family
of those who follow you,
for they are family to us
and give us help and encouragement
as we also try to follow you.

Five: Simon of Cyrene helps carry the cross

Jesus struggled once again with the cross.

The guard grew impatient with his slowness.

They saw a strongly built man coming in from the country, Simon of Cyrene.

'Here, you, carry the cross for the wretched prisoner,' the soldiers commanded.

So Simon did.

Dear God,
Thank you for those whom we do not know
who help us with their greater strength
when we are in need.

Six: Veronica wipes the face of Jesus

Jesus could barely see the way ahead.
    Tears clouded his eyes.
    He tried to wipe them, but only smeared
them with the dust from his hands.
    Then a woman stepped forward,
and gently she wiped his face with a cloth.

Dear God,
We thank you for those who see
the little ways in which to give
help and support.

Seven: Jesus falls the second time

The guard urged Jesus forward, for his sentence
had to be carried out without delay.

But who can walk calmly to the place where
there will be pain and punishment?

Once again, Jesus fell.

Dear God,
I try to follow Jesus
but sometimes I grow fearful and discouraged.
Help me to trust
that in your care
all things will work together
for the good.

Eight: The women of Jerusalem mourn for Jesus

A group of women wept to see Jesus so cruelly treated.

'He has done no wrong,' they cried. 'What is happening is neither right nor fair.'

Jesus looked at them sadly.

'Do not weep for me,' he said. 'Weep for yourselves and for your children who have to go on living in these troubled times.'

Dear God,
When the world is unkind
and people are so unfair,
we weep with you;
you weep for us.

Nine: Jesus falls the third time

Jesus and the guard approached the hill
that was to be the end of the journey.
Shaking with fear, Jesus fell again.

Dear God,
Whenever in this world
there is more suffering
than goodness,
help me to believe
that your goodness is strong
and your love is for ever.

Ten: Jesus is stripped of his garments

At the place of execution the guards took from Jesus
even the clothes he was wearing.

They gambled among themselves to decide who
would have his tunic.

Jesus was left with nothing.

Dear God,
Help me not to worry
about the things that people can steal,
but rather to seek to live in the way you want,
to live in your kingdom.

Eleven: Jesus is nailed to the cross

Then the guards laid Jesus on the cross and hammered iron nails through his hands and his feet.

They hung him up to die while others mocked at his suffering.

Dear God,
When I see violent people win,
may I continue
to believe in peace.

Twelve: Jesus dies upon the cross

For several hours, Jesus hung upon the cross.
He asked God to forgive those who had
treated him so cruelly.
He asked his friend, John, to be a son to his mother.
He pleaded with God to tell him why he had been
left alone to suffer.
And then he died.

Dear God,
In the face of death,
may I continue to believe
that you give life.

Thirteen: The body of Jesus is taken down from the cross

A man named Joseph, from the town of Arimathea, saw Jesus die. He was a wealthy man and had been a secret follower of Jesus. He asked Pilate if he could take the body and give it a proper burial.

Dear God,
May we continue to do good
even when it seems that we
have nothing left to hope for.

Fourteen: The body of Jesus is laid in the tomb

Joseph had had a tomb prepared for his own death: a low cave cut into the rock with a large round stone to roll in place as a door.

As evening fell, Joseph and some of Jesus' friends hurriedly wrapped the body and laid it inside with the door rolled shut.

Then, they had to hurry home because their weekly day of rest, the Sabbath, was beginning.

Dear God,
When we are in despair
and we have too many hours
to sit and weep,
be with us.

Fifteen: Jesus rises from the tomb

When the day of rest was over, some women who had been followers of Jesus returned to the tomb.

They brought with them spices, to prepare the body properly for burial according to their traditions.

As they approached, they saw that the stone was rolled aside.

The body was no longer inside. Instead, they saw angels.

'Why are you looking among the dead for someone who is alive?' asked the angels.

'Jesus is not here: he is risen.'

Dear God,
Help us to believe in you
and in the love that will bring us
to everlasting life.

The story continues

'He is not here. He is risen!'

The women could hardly believe the angels' words. They ran to tell the disciples the astonishing news.

At first, no one believed what they said. Yet the tomb was certainly empty.

Then Jesus came and met with his friends: they saw him and they touched him.

So it continued for forty days, and then Jesus' friends saw him being taken up to heaven.

Soon afterwards, they began to tell the world the story of Jesus, the story of the cross.

There is a part of the story when wicked and cruel people seem to be winning. Then God changes everything, bringing life and love that will never end.

Here is what one of Jesus' followers wrote to his friends:

'Dear friends, let us love one another, because love comes from God. Whoever loves is a child of God and knows God. Whoever does not love does not know God, for God is love. And God showed his love for us by sending his only Son into the world, so that we might have life through him. This is what love is: it is not that we have loved God, but that he loved us and sent his Son to be the means by which our sins are forgiven.'

1 John 4:7–10

Thanks be to thee,
Lord Jesus Christ,
for all the benefits
which thou hast won for us,
for all the pains and insults
which thou hast borne for us.

O most merciful redeemer,
friend and brother,
may we know thee more clearly,
love thee more dearly,
and follow thee more nearly,
day by day.

Richard of Chichester (1197–1253)